Dog Breeds Pictures

by

Eric Nolah

Also by Eric Nolah

Choosing a Dog Breed Guide
ISBN 978-0-9866004-5-6

Cute Puppy Pictures
ISBN 978-0-9866004-7-0

Dog Breeds Pictures
by Eric Nolah

ISBN 978-0-9866004-6-3

Printed in the United States of America

For David

Afghan Hound

Origin: Afghanistan
Weight (male): 20-27 kg (45-60 lb)
Height (male): 61–73 cm (24–29 in)
Coat: long and fine
Life span: 11-13 years

Airedale Terrier

Origin: England
Weight (male): 25–30 Kg (55–66 lb)
Height (male): 58–61 cm (23–24 in)
Coat: hard, dense and wiry
Life span: 11-12 years

Akita Inu

Origin: Japan
Weight (male): 34–54 kg (75–119 lb)
Height (male): 61–66 cm (24–26 in)
Coat: coarse, straight, with soft undercoat
Life span: 11–15 years

Alaskan Malamute

Origin: United States (Alaska)
Weight (male): 34–41 kg (75–90 lb)
Height (male): 63–65 cm (25–26 in)
Coat: thick, a double coat, with plush undercoat
Life span: up to 14 years

American Bulldog

Origin: United States
Weight (male): 27-60 kg (70-120 lb)
Height (male): 50-71 cm (20-27 in)
Coat: short, harsh
Life span: 10-12 years

American Cocker Spaniel

Origin: United States
Weight (male): 11-15 kg (24-33 lb)
Height (male): 34-39 cm (13.5-15.5 in)
Coat: silky and flat
Life span: 10-11 years

American Eskimo Dog

Origin: United States
Weight (male): 11-18 kg (25-40 lb)
Height (male): 40-48 cm (16-19 in)
Coat: heavy around the neck, creating a ruff or mane
Life span: 12-13 years

American Pit Bull Terrier

Origin: United States
Weight (male): 16-27 kg (35-60 lb)
Height (male): 46-61 cm (18-24 in)
Coat: short
Life span: 11-12 years

Anatolian Shepherd

Origin: Turkey
Weight (male): 41-68 kg (90-150 lb)
Height (male): 74-91 cm (29-36 in)
Coat: somewhat wirey
Life span: 12-15 years

Argentine Dogo

Origin: Argentina
Weight (male): 36-45 kg (80-100 lb)
Height (male): 62-68 cm (24-27 in)
Coat: thick, glossy
Life span: 10-12 years

Australian Shepherd

Origin: United States
Weight (male): 25-29 kg (50-65 lb)
Height (male): 53-58 cm (21-23 in)
Coat: straight and may have curls
Life span: 12-15 years

Beagle

Origin: England
Weight (male): 8-16 kg (18-35 lb)
Height (male): 33-41 cm (13-16 in)
Coat: medium length, close, hard and sleek
Life span: 12-15 years

Bearded Collie

Origin: Scotland
Weight (male): 18-27 kg (40-60 lb)
Height (male): 51-56 cm (20-22 in)
Coat: shaggy, waterproof, hangs over the entire body including the chin
Life span: 14-15 years

Beauceron

Origin: France
Weight (male): 32-45 kg (70-100 lb)
Height (male): 65-70 cm (26-28 in)
Coat: harsh outer coat with woolly, fluffy under-coat
Life span: 10-13 years

Belgian Shepherd

Origin: Belgium
Weight (male): 29-34 kg (65-75 lb)
Height (male): 61-66 cm (24-26 in)
Coat: long, well fitting, straight and abundant hairs
Life span: 12-14 years

Bernese Mountain Dog

Origin: Switzerland
Weight (male): 38-50 kg (85-110 lb)
Height (male): 61-71 cm (24-28 in)
Coat: tricolor with symmetrical markings of black, rust and white
Life span: 6-8 years

Border Collie

Origin: Scotland, England, Wales
Weight (male): 14-20 kg (30-45 lb)
Height (male): 48-56 cm (19-22 in)
Coat: weather resistant, dense and close-fitting
Life span: 10-15 years

Border Terrier

Origin: Scotland, England
Weight (male): 6-7 kg (13-16 lb)
Height (male): 33-41 cm (13-16 in)
Coat: short, dense, wiry, double coat
Life span: 15+ years

Borzoi

Origin: Russia
Weight (male): 34-48 kg (70-105 lb)
Height (male): 80+ cm (30+ in)
Coat: can vary from long and silky to coarse and curly
Life span: 7-10 years

Boston Terrier

Origin: United States
Weight (male): 4-11 kg (9-25 lb)
Height (male): 38-43 cm (15-17 in)
Coat: short, fine textured
Life span: 15+ years

Boxer

Origin: Germany
Weight (male): 29-45 kg (65-99 lb)
Height (male): 56-63 cm (22-25 in)
Coat: short, shiny, smooth, close-lying
Life span: 10-12 years

Braque d'Auvergne

Origin: France
Weight (male): 22-28 kg (49-62 lb)
Height (male): 53-63 cm (22-25 in)
Coat: short, fine and shiny
Life span: 12-13 years

Briard

Origin: France
Weight (male): 30-40 kg (66-88 lb)
Height (male): 58-69 cm (22-27 in)
Coat: course, hard and dry
Life span: 10-12 years

Brittany
(Epagneul Breton)

Origin: France
Weight (male): 16-25 kg (35-55 lb)
Height (male): 43-53 cm (17-21 in)
Coat: medium length flowing
Life span: 10-12 years

Brussels Griffon

Origin: Belgium
Weight (male): 2.5-5.5 kg (6-12 lb)
Height (male): 18-20 cm (7-8 in)
Coat: dense and wiry
Life span: 12-15 years

Bull Terrier

Origin: England
Weight (male): 20-38 kg (44-85 lb)
Height (male): 51-61 cm (20-24 in)
Coat: short, dense
Life span: 10-12 years

Bullmastiff

Origin: England
Weight (male): 50-59 kg (110-130 lb)
Height (male): 63-69 cm (25-27 in)
Coat: short, dense, slightly rough
Life span: 8-10 years

Cane Corso

Origin: Italy
Weight (male): 45-50 kg (99-110 lb)
Height (male): 64-68 cm (25-27 in)
Coat: short hair but not smooth
Life span: 10-11 years

Catalan Sheepdog

Origin: Spain
Weight (male): 18-20 kg (39-44 lb)
Height (male): 45-55 cm (18-22 in)
Coat: long, smooth, straight and slightly wavy
Life span: 12-14 years

Cavalier King Charles Spaniel

Origin: England
Weight (male): 6-8 kg (13-18 lb)
Height (male): 30-33 cm (12-13 in)
Coat: silky, medium in length
Life span: 9-14 years

Chihuahua

Origin: Mexico
Weight (male): 1-3 kg (2-6 lb)
Height (male): 15-23 cm (6-9 in)
Coat: short coat or long, wavy or flat coat
Life span: 14-18 years

Chinese Crested Dog

Origin: China
Weight (male): 2.5-4.5 kg (5-10 lb)
Height (male): 28-33 cm (11-13 in)
Coat: two very distinct coat types: hairless or full, thick and long coat of fine, silky hair
Life span: 10-12 years

Chow Chow

Origin: China
Weight (male): 25-32 kg (55-70 lb)
Height (male): 48-56 cm (19-22 in)
Coat: thick and coarse
Life span: 9-15 years

Dachshund

Origin: China
Weight (male): 7-13 kg (15-28 lb)
Height (male): 20-27 cm (8-11 in)
Coat: three coat varieties: smooth coat (short hair), long hair, and wire-hair
Life span: 12-15 years

Dalmatian

Origin: Croatia
Weight (male): 16-30 kg (35-65 lb)
Height (male): 50-60 cm (22-24 in)
Coat: white background
Life span: 12-14 years

Doberman Pinscher

Origin: Germany
Weight (male): 35-45 kg (75-100 lb)
Height (male): 66-71 cm (26-28 in)
Coat: short, hard, thick
Life span: 9-10 years

Dogue de Bordeaux

Origin: France
Weight (male): 54-65 kg (120-145 lb)
Height (male): 58-75 cm (23-30 in)
Coat: short, fine, and soft to the touch
Life span: 7-10 years

English Cocker Spaniel

Origin: England
Weight (male): 13-16 kg (28-34 lb)
Height (male): 38-43 cm (15-17 in)
Coat: black, red or liver
Life span: 12-15 years

English Foxhound

Origin: England
Weight (male): 29-32 kg (65-70 lb)
Height (male): 56-63 cm (22-25 in)
Coat: short, hard, dense and glossy
Life span: 10-13 years

English Springer Spaniel

Origin: England
Weight (male): 20-25 kg (45-55 lb)
Height (male): 48-56 cm (19-21 in)
Coat: medium in length with feathering over the legs, ears, cheeks and brisket
Life span: 12-14 years

Entlebucher Mountain Dog

Origin: Switzerland
Weight (male): 20-30 kg (45-65 lb)
Height (male): 48-51 cm (19-20 in)
Coat: short, hard, dense and glossy
Life span: 11-15 years

Eurasier

Origin: Germany
Weight (male): 23-32 kg (51-71 lb)
Height (male): 52-60 cm (20-24 in)
Coat: long, thick double coat
Life span: 11-13 years

Finnish Spitz

Origin: Finland
Weight (male): 11-13 kg (27-33 lb)
Height (male): 44-50 cm (16-19 in)
Coat: reddish-brown, red gold on back, preferably bright; lighter shades permissible on the underside
Life span: 12-15 years

French Bulldog

Origin: England
Weight (male): 9-13 kg (19-28 lb)
Height (male): 28-30 cm (11-12 in)
Coat: brindle, pied or fawn
Life span: 10-12 years

Galgo Español

Origin: Spain
Weight (male): 27-30 kg (60-65 lb)
Height (male): 66-71 cm (26-28 in)
Coat: smooth, or rough
Life span: 12-15 years

German Shepherd

Origin: Germany
Weight (male): 30–40 kg (66–88 lb)
Height (male): 60–65 cm (24–26 in)
Coat: dense, woolly underhair and a medium-length, harsh, straight or slightly wavy outercoat
Life span: 7-10 years

German Shorthaired Pointer

Origin: Germany
Weight (male): 25-32 kg (55-70 lb)
Height (male): 58-63 cm (23-25 in)
Coat: short, harsh, wiry, flat, thick
Life span: 12-14 years

Giant Schnauzer

Origin: Germany
Weight (male): 31-36 kg (70-80 lb)
Height (male): 64-71 cm (25-28 in)
Coat: double coated, outercoat-wiry, dense, bushy, thick, hard, harsh, undercoat-soft
Life span: 11-12 years

Golden Retriever

Origin: Scotland
Weight (male): 27-36 kg (60-80 lb)
Height (male): 56-61 cm (22-24 in)
Coat: golden yellow
Life span: 10-12 years

Great Dane

Origin: Denmark or Germany
Weight (male): 54-90 kg (120-200 lb)
Height (male): 76-86 cm (30-34 in)
Coat: smooth short-haired coat
Life span: under 10 years

Greater Swiss Mountain Dog

Origin: Switzerland
Weight (male): 45-59 kg (100-130 lb)
Height (male): 65-72 cm (25-28 in)
Coat: double coat
Life span: 8-11 years

Greyhound

Origin: Egypt
Weight (male): 27-40 kg (60-88 lb)
Height (male): 71-76 cm (28-30 in)
Coat: fine, smooth
Life span: 10-13 years

Havanese

Origin: Western Mediterranean Region
Weight (male): 3-6 kg (7-13 lb)
Height (male): 20-28 cm (8-11 in)
Coat: long hairs colores in white, black, brown and gray
Life span: 14-15 years

Hovawart

Origin: Germany
Weight (male): 25-51 kg (55-90 lb)
Height (male): 58-70 cm (23-28 in)
Coat: black, black and gold, and blond long hairs
Life span: 11-15 years

Irish Setter

Origin: Ireland
Weight (male): 29-34 kg (65-75 lb)
Height (male): 66-71 cm (26-28 in)
Coat: coat is moderately long and silky and of a deep red color
Life span: 11-15 years

Jack Russell Terrier

Origin: England
Weight (male): 6-8 kg (14-18 lb)
Height (male): 25-38 cm (10-15 in)
Coat: short-haired and has various colors liek black, white, brown, golden yellow combinations
Life span: 15-17 years

Japanese Bandog Tosa Inu

Origin: Japan
Weight (male): 40-77 kg (90-170 lb)
Height (male): 61-68 cm (24-27 in)
Coat: short-haired and usually has brown and black colors
Life span: 10-12 years

Japanese Chin

Origin: Japan
Weight (male): 2-7 kg (4-15 lb)
Height (male): 18-28 cm (7-11 in)
Coat: long-haired and typically colored in white, black and brown
Life span: under 10 years

Keeshond

Origin: Netherlands, Germany
Weight (male): 25-30 kg (55-66 lb)
Height (male): 44-48 cm (17-19 in)
Coat: long-haired and usually colored in gray, brown and black
Life span: 12-15 years

Kooikerhondje

Origin: Netherlands
Weight (male): 9-18 kg (20-40 lb)
Height (male): 36-41 cm (14-16 in)
Coat: semi-long hairs and usually colored in white, golden yellow, brown and black
Life span: 12-14 years

Labrador

Origin: Canada
Weight (male): 27–36 kg (60–79 lb)
Height (male): 56–70 cm (22–28 in)
Coat: smooth, short and dense straight hair
Life span: 10-12 years

Leonberger

Origin: Germany
Weight (male): 59-77 kg (130-170 lb)
Height (male): 74-80 cm (29-31 in)
Coat: semi-long haired and usually colored in brown and black combination
Life span: 8-9 years

Lhasa Apso

Origin: Tibet
Weight (male): 6-7 kg (13-15 lb)
Height (male): 25-28 cm (10-11 in)
Coat: fine long hairs and usually colored in gray, golden yellow, brown, black and white combinations
Life span: 15-18 years

Löwchen

Origin: Germany, France, Netherlands, Spain
Weight (male): 4-8 kg (9-18 lb)
Height (male): 25-33 cm (10-13 in)
Coat: silky lion coat
Life span: 12-14 years

Maltese

Origin: Italy
Weight (male): 2-3 kg (4-7 lb)
Height (male): 20-25 cm (8-10 in)
Coat: white
Life span: 12-14 years

Manchester Terrier

Origin: England
Weight (male): 2.5-3.5 kg (6-8 lb)
Height (male): 25-30 cm (10-12 in)
Coat: short-haired and usually black in color
Life span: 15 or more years

Miniature Pinscher

Origin: Germany
Weight (male): 4-5 kg (8-10 lb)
Height (male): 25-30 cm (10-12 in)
Coat: smooth and short haired
Life span: 15 or more years

Newfoundland Dog

Origin: Canada
Weight (male): 59-68 kg (130-150 lb)
Height (male): 69-74 cm (27-29 in)
Coat: thick and straight
Life span: 8-13 years

Nova Scotia Toller

Origin: Canada
Weight (male): 17-23 kg (37-51 lb)
Height (male): 43-53 cm (17-21 in)
Coat: water-repellent, double coat
Life span: 12-14 years

Old English Sheepdog

Origin: England
Weight (male): 36–46 kg (79–100 lb)
Height (male): 56-61 cm (22-24 in)
Coat: long fine haired
Life span: 10-12 years

Papillon

Origin: Spain, Belgium, France
Weight (male): 4-5 kg (8-10 lb)
Height (male): 20-28 cm (8-11 in)
Coat: long, silky, single coat
Life span: 14-16 years

Parson Russell Terrier

Origin: England
Weight (male): 6-8 kg (14-18 lb)
Height (male): 31-36 cm (12-14 in)
Coat: single and short-haired
Life span: 15 or more years

Pekingese

Origin: China
Weight (male): 3.6-4.5 kg (8-10 lb)
Height (male): 30-45 cm (6-9 in)
Coat: very long, double coat
Life span: 10-15 years

Peruvian Hairless Dog

Origin: Peru
Weight (male): 12-23 kg (26-50 lb)
Height (male): 50-65 cm (20-26 in)
Coat: may have short hair on top of its head, on its feet, and on the tip of its tail
Life span: 11-12 years

Polish Lowland Sheepdog

Origin: Poland
Weight (male): 14-16 kg (30-35 lb)
Height (male): 41-5 cm (16-20 in)
Coat: long wire-haired coat
Life span: 12-15 years

Pomeranian

Origin: Germany, Poland
Weight (male): 1-3 kg (3-7 lb)
Height (male): 18-30 cm (7-12 in)
Coat: very long, double coat
Life span: about 15 years

Poodle

Origin: Germany, France
Weight (male): 7-8 kg (15-17 lb)
Height (male): 28-38 cm (11-15 in)
Coat: long curly haired
Life span: 12-15 years

Pug

Origin: China
Weight (male): 25-30 kg (10-12 lb)
Height (male): 30-36 cm (12-14 in)
Coat: smooth, short-haired coat is easy to groom
Life span: 12-15 years

Pyrenean Shepherd

Origin: France
Weight (male): 7-14 kg (15-30 lb)
Height (male): 38-53 cm (15-21 in)
Coat: smooth faced
Life span: about 15 years

Rhodesian Ridgeback

Origin: Rhodesia
Weight (male): 36-41 kg (80-90 lb)
Height (male): 63-69 cm (25-27in)
Coat: smooth, short-haired coat
Life span: 10-12 years

Rottweiler

Origin: Germany
Weight (male): 50-60 kg (110-130 lb)
Height (male): 61-69 cm (24-27 in)
Coat: double coated, short, hard and thick
Life span: 9-12 years

Rough Collie

Origin: Scotland
Weight (male): 27-34 kg (60-75 lb)
Height (male): 61-66 cm (24-26 in)
Coat: stiff
Life span: 14-16 years

Saarlooswolfhond

Origin: Netherlands, Germany
Weight (male): 36-41 kg (79-90 lb)
Height (male): 60-75 cm (24-29 in)
Coat: weather resistant
Life span: 10-12 years

Saint Bernard

Origin: Italy, Switzerland
Weight (male): 50-91 kg (110-200 lb)
Height (male): 61-70 cm (25-27 in)
Coat: thick and stiff
Life span: 8-10 years

Samoyed

Origin: Russia
Weight (male): 20-30 kg (45-65 lb)
Height (male): 53-60 cm (21-23 in)
Coat: long ang stiff hair
Life span: 12-15 years

Schipperke

Origin: Belgium
Weight (male): 5-8 kg (12-18 lb)
Height (male): 21-33 cm (10-13 in)
Coat: very clean and pretty much takes care of its own grooming
Life span: 15 or more years

Scottish Terrier

Origin: Scotland
Weight (male): 8-10 kg (19-23 lb)
Height (male): 25-28 cm (10-11 in)
Coat: harsh wiry coat
Life span: 12-15 years

Shar Pei

Origin: China
Weight (male): 23-30 kg (55-65 lb)
Height (male): 46-51 cm (18-20 in)
Coat: short and stiff
Life span: 7-15 years

Shetland Sheepdog

Origin: Scotland
Weight (male): 6-12 kg (14-27 lb)
Height (male): 33-41 cm (13-16 in)
Coat: long and fine hair
Life span: 12-15 years

Shih Tzu

Origin: Switzerland
Weight (male): 4-7 kg (9-16 lb)
Height (male): 20–28 cm (8-11 in)
Coat: dense and long
Life span: 14-18 years

Small Munsterlander

Origin: Germany
Weight (male): 4-7 kg (9-16 lb)
Height (male): 20-28 cm (8-11 in)
Coat: soft, medium length
Life span: 14-18 years

Soft-Coated Wheaten Terrier

Origin: Ireland
Weight (male): 16-20 kg (35-45 lb)
Height (male): 43-51 cm (17-20 in)
Coat: soft and silky, loosely waved or curly
Life span: 12-15 years

Spanish Water Dog

Origin: Spain
Weight (male): 18-22 kg (40-49 lb)
Height (male): 44-50 cm (17-20 in)
Coat: stif, thick and curly hairs
Life span: 10-14 years

Staffordshire Bull Terrier

Origin: England
Weight (male): 11-17 kg (25-38 lb)
Height (male): 36-41 cm (14-16 in)
Coat: smooth, short-haired coat
Life span: 10-16 years

Tibetan Mastiff

Origin: China
Weight (male): 64-78 kg (140-170 lb)
Height (male): 61-71 cm (25-28 in)
Coat: thick and stiff hair
Life span: 15 or more years

Tibetan Spaniel

Origin: Tibet
Weight (male): 4-7 kg (9-15 lb)
Height (male): about 25 cm (10 in)
Coat: long and silky hairs
Life span: 12-15 years

Tibetan Terrier

Origin: Tibet
Weight (male): 8-14 kg (18-30 lb)
Height (male): 36-43 cm (14-17 in)
Coat: long and thick hair
Life span: 12-15 years

Toy Fox Terrier

Origin: United States
Weight (male): 1.5-3 kg (3-7 lb)
Height (male): about 25 cm (10 in)
Coat: short and fine hairs
Life span: 13-14 years

Vizsla

Origin: Hungary
Weight (male): 20-27 kg (45-60 lb)
Height (male): 56-66 cm (22-26 in)
Coat: smooth, short-haired coat
Life span: 12-15 years

Weimaraner

Origin: Germany
Weight (male): 25-32 kg (55-70 lb)
Height (male): 61-69 cm (24-27 in)
Coat: smooth, short-haired coat
Life span: 10-12 years

Welsh Corgi

Origin: Wales
Weight (male): about 12 kg (27 lb)
Height (male): 25-33 cm (10-13 in)
Coat: short or medium length, hard textured, weatherproof with a good undercoat
Life span: 12-14 years

West Highland White Terrier

Origin: Scotland
Weight (male): 7-10 kg (15-22 lb)
Height (male): 25-30 cm (10-12 in)
Coat: harsh, straight, short-haired double coat
Life span: 15 or more years

Whippet

Origin: England
Weight (male): 7-14 kg (15–30 lb)
Height (male): 47-57 cm (18-22 in)
Coat: fine, dense
Life span: 12-15 years

White English Bulldog

Origin: United States
Weight (male): 29-50 kg (65-11- lb)
Height (male): 53-63 cm (21-25 in)
Coat: short and stiff
Life span: 10-13 years

Yorkshire Terrier

Origin: England
Weight (male): about 3 kg (7 lb)
Height (male): 15-17 cm (6-7 in)
Coat: Silky and fine
Life span: 13-16 years

Where to Buy this Book

You can buy this book on Amazon. Just go to amazon.com (or your local Amazon site if available) and search for "Dog Breeds Pictures by Eric Nolah" or just "Eric Nolah".

You can also order it at any bookstore if they don't have it in stock. Just give them the IBSN below:

ISBN 978-0-9866004-6-3

Also by Eric Nolah

Choosing a Dog Breed Guide
ISBN 978-0-9866004-5-6

Cute Puppy Pictures
ISBN 978-0-9866004-7-0

CPSIA information can be obtained
at www.ICGtesting.com
Printed in the USA
LVIW011900250712
291475LV00001BA